The
World's Best
Boss Jokes

In this series

The World's Best Boss Jokes

Edward Phillips

Illustrations by Noel Ford

HarperCollins*Publishers*

HarperCollins*Publishers*
77–85 Fulham Palace Road,
Hammersmith, London W6 8JB

A Paperback Original 1994
1 3 5 7 9 8 6 4 2

A catalogue record for this book
is available from the British Library

ISBN 0 00 638241 X

Set in Goudy Old Style by
Avocet Typesetters, Bicester, Oxon

Printed in Great Britain by
HarperCollinsManufacturing Glasgow

The chief buyer of a large London fashion house went into her boss's office to ask for a raise. 'Impossible!' said the boss. 'I'm already paying you more than any of the male executives and most of them have a wife and several children to support.'

'I was under the impression,' she said icily, 'that we got paid for what we produce at work – not what we produce at home.'

The chairman of a large company discovered that the office boy had been pilfering from the petty cash. The managing director was all in favour of calling in the police, but the chairman took a more enlightened view. 'Let us remember,' he said, 'that we began in a small way ourselves.'

The boss of a large company was frantic. He and his partner were the only ones who knew the combination to the office safe; he had forgotten it and his partner was away on a six-week cruise and couldn't be reached. At the end of the fourth week, his partner called him from Singapore. 'Thank God you called!' said the boss. 'I forgot the combination to the safe! We've done no business for weeks! I've had to lay people off, the sales force is sitting around doing nothing – and I'm even having to turn down orders from some of our biggest customers!'

'But it's so easy,' said his partner. 'You just turn once to the right and twice to the left.'

'But what about the combination?' yelled the boss. 'I can't remember the numbers!'

'The numbers don't matter,' said his partner. 'The lock's broken anyway.'

'You're late,' said the boss to his secretary when she strolled in at 10 a.m.

'I'm not really late, sir,' she said. 'I just took my coffee break before I came in.'

The son of a rather shady company chairman was asked by his mathematics teacher, 'If your father borrowed £250,000 from his bank and promised payment on the loan at £50,000 per month, how much would he owe at the end of one month?'

'£250,000,' said the boy.

'You obviously don't know much about mathematics,' said the teacher.

'And you obviously don't know much about my father,' replied the boy.

One of the most famous bosses the world has ever known is Henry Ford, the American car manufacturer. On one of his visits to this country, he was approached in the Savoy Grill by a young man who said, 'Excuse me, Mr Ford, you don't know me – and this is an awful cheek – but I wonder if you would do me a small favour. Oh, I don't want to borrow money or anything like that. It's just that I'm meeting some friends here for lunch tomorrow and they're all pretty successful businessmen – and I just thought that if you could come up to us and just casually say, "Good morning, Bill", well, it might do me a bit of good.'

This idea appealed to Ford's sense of humour and he readily agreed to the plan. So the next day, just before lunch, he entered the Savoy Grill and immediately spotted young Bill at the bar, in the company of a number of distinguished-looking businessmen. He walked up to the group and said enthusiastically, 'Hello, Bill! How are you?'

The young man looked at him coldly and said, 'Push off, Henry – can't you see I'm busy!'

The boss called the office manager into his office and was closeted with him for several minutes. Then he called in the personnel manager and shortly after that, the sales manager. One by one, he summoned all the male executives and finally the office boy was called in. Looking at him sternly, the boss said, 'Have you been having an affair with my secretary?'

'No, sir!' stammered the office boy. 'Certainly not!'

Obviously relieved, the boss said, 'Good! Now will you please go to her office and tell her she's fired!'

The new recruit to the typing pool asked the supervisor where the 'Ladies' was. 'Go through here to the General Office,' said the supervisor, 'and keep going until you see a red-haired young man who winks at you. Continue on through until you come to a hoarse voice that will say "Wow!", then turn right until you run into a low whistle and you're there.'

Two small-time businessmen met in a pub. They were well known for dealing in everything and anything, and one of them said to the other in a confidential whisper: 'Would you like to buy an African elephant for £100?'

'Are you crazy?' said the second man. 'I live in a tower block and I've got four kids!'

'All right, keep your voice down!' said the first businessman. 'Tell you what I'll do. I can let you have two African elephants for £150.'

'Ah!' said his friend. 'Now you're talking!'

The managing director of a large company had been invited to dinner by an old friend. His host, who was of a religious turn of mind, asked his guest if he would say grace. The boss was a little put out at this but he put his hands together and said, 'O Lord, we are in receipt of your kind favours of recent date for which we thank you. We trust that we may continue to merit your confidence and that we shall be able to look forward to receiving your esteemed blessings in the foreseeable future. Yours obediently. Amen.'

FIRST BOSS: 'How's business?'
SECOND BOSS: 'Pretty good! One of our men got a £50,000 order yesterday.'
FIRST BOSS: '£50,000! I don't believe it!'
SECOND BOSS: 'It's true! Look — here's the cancellation!'

The little office clerk crept meekly into the boss's office. 'Excuse me, sir,' he said. 'I'm sorry to bother you, but my wife told me that I had to ask you for a raise.'

'I see,' said the boss. 'All right — I'll ask my wife if I can give you one.'

'Will you ever forget that lovely weekend we had together on the French Riviera?' the boss asked his beautiful secretary.

'What's it worth?' she said slyly.

The boss was addressing a meeting of the firm's senior executives and sales staff. 'Now, when my son starts work here on Monday morning,' he said, 'I want you to treat him just as you would treat any other new employee who was going to take over the company in two years' time.'

P.D. Armour, the great American meat magnate, was a stickler for hard work and long hours. He once hired a new clerk but forgot to tell him what time he was expected to report for work. On the first day, the new clerk turned up at 8 a.m. Armour and his staff were already hard at work.

The next day, the clerk came in at 7.30 a.m. — only to find once again that Armour and his staff were already on the job. Armour glowered at him but said nothing.

On the third morning, the new employee managed to get in at 7 a.m. Everybody was already there. Armour looked up from his desk and said, 'Young man — just what is it you do with your mornings?'

A large firm of importers was in need of a qualified accountant to take over the financial side of the business. The managing director insisted that they hire only a one-armed man. 'Why on earth should we hire a one-armed man?' asked the puzzled personnel manager.

'Because,' said the managing director, 'I'm fed up with always getting financial advice which begins, "Well, on the one hand . . . but then again, on the other hand . . ." '

'Briggs,' said the boss one morning, 'I just don't know how we're going to get along without you – but starting Monday, we're going to try.'

Some bosses really know how to annoy their secretaries, like the one who said, 'Miss Somers, please make a dozen copies of this and circulate the one with the fewest mistakes.'

The boss had a long and important letter to dictate, but he didn't get round to it until nearly 4.45. His secretary wasn't able to finish it until gone 7 p.m. Thoroughly annoyed, she handed the letter over for signature and remarked, 'I just wish I could be the boss for a week and let you be the secretary!'

'I don't think that would work,' said the boss. 'I could never drink that much coffee.'

The new typist was so sweet and pleasant that the boss didn't have the heart to tell her off about her spelling mistakes, her sloppy typing and her general inefficiency. One morning he saw her searching frantically through the filing cabinets and cupboards, with tears streaming down her face. 'Come, come,' he said soothingly. 'Whatever it is you've lost, it can't be so important that you should get this upset about it.'

'It is!' she sobbed. 'It's my lunch!'

The managing director of a merchant banker's firm in the City recently circulated the following memo to all staff:

I am instituting a new system in the company which we shall refer to as the Work Period. I am asking that all employees will endeavour to find some time during the day to implement Work Periods – without, of course, infringing on coffee breaks, lunch hours, rest periods, selling raffle tickets, taking up office collections and planning holidays.

WIFE: 'Did you have a good afternoon on the golf course, dear?'

HUSBAND: 'Not bad.'

WIFE: 'And did you win?'

HUSBAND: 'Don't be silly. I was playing the boss.'

A top executive was lunching with his friend at his club. 'I made a bad mistake a couple of months ago,' he said. 'I loaned an associate £5,000 and now I can't get him to repay the loan. And what's even worse, I didn't get any form of receipt for the loan.'

'Well,' said his friend, 'I suggest you write to him and ask him for immediate repayment of the £10,000.'

'It wasn't £10,000,' said the executive. 'I just told you – it was £5,000.'

'I know,' said his friend. 'So he'll write back and tell you it was only £5,000 and then you'll have your receipt.'

The boss of a large manufacturing company recently circulated the following memo to all junior executives:

Assistant managers, deputy managers and junior departmental heads who have no personal secretaries should take advantage of the female staff in the typing pool.

A top executive has been defined as a man who can take as long as he wants to make a snap decision.

The manager of a construction company recently received an urgent phone call from one of his site bosses. 'Chief, we're in trouble,' said the site boss. 'It's those two show houses in Princess Road. We removed the scaffolding this morning and both houses fell down!'

'I've told you a hundred times!' stormed the boss. 'Don't take the scaffolding down until you've put the wallpaper up!'

'What is business ethics, Dad?' asked the young son of one of the bosses of a large clothing store.

'I'll give you an example,' said his father. 'A customer came in yesterday and bought some shirts. I was in the store and I served him personally. He paid with a £50 note and as I was putting it in the till I saw that he had given me two £50 notes stuck together. Now this is where business ethics come in. Should I tell my partner or not?'

A new chauffeur for the managing director reported for work one Monday morning. As the boss climbed into the back of the Rolls-Royce, he said, 'What's your name, driver?'

'Henry, sir,' said the chauffeur.

'I don't call my chauffeur by his Christian name,' said the boss huffily. 'What's your surname?'

'Darling, sir.'

'Very well then, Henry – drive on,' said the boss.

The boss called his top executive into his office and said, 'Wilkins, I've been watching you carefully over the last few months. You're hard-working, industrious, efficient – and you've made it your business to find out everything about the company's affairs, down to the smallest detail. Consequently, you're fired. It's men like you who resign and go off to start rival companies!'

The manager called his assistant into the office and closed the door sternly. 'Now listen to me,' he said. 'There's £50 missing from the petty cash box. There are only two keys to that box. I have one and you have the other.'

'Well,' said the assistant, 'suppose we each put in £25 and say no more about it?'

The boss had been married just over a year. Now he stood in the bedroom gazing down in wonder at the cot where his new baby son lay sleeping peacefully. 'A penny for your thoughts, dear,' said his wife in a soft voice.

'I was just wondering,' said the boss, 'how on earth they can turn out a cot like that for only £49.50!'

A pretty young secretary walked into her boss's office one morning and said, 'I've got some good news and some bad news.'

'Look, I'm very busy this morning,' said the boss. 'I haven't got time to mess about — just tell me the good news.'

'Well,' said his secretary, 'the good news is that you're not sterile.'

A very junior civil servant found that the confidential minutes of a top secret Cabinet meeting had been delivered to his desk. He read through them, initialled them and returned them.

The following morning, the documents were returned to him from his boss with a note attached which read: *'It is noted* that you have read and initialled these minutes. As you do not have security clearance for confidential documents of this type, kindly delete your initials and return the document.' The clerk complied with this request.

The next morning, he found that his boss had returned the minutes once again with the following memo attached: 'It is noted that you have made an alteration to the attached documents. Kindly initial the alteration and return.'

Said the foreman of a lumber company to an applicant for a tree-felling job: 'Where did you learn to chop down trees?'

'In the Sahara,' said the lad.

'The Sahara? There are no trees in the Sahara!'

'No,' said the lad. 'Not now there aren't.'

Remember, the boss is not always right; but he is always the boss.

SECRETARY: 'Excuse me, sir, I think you're wanted on the phone.'

BOSS: 'What do you mean "you think" I'm wanted on the phone? Either I am or I'm not!'

SECRETARY: 'Well, sir, the caller said, "Is that stupid old idiot in yet?" '

A City businessman began dating his secretary and decided that she would make an ideal wife. Being in the insurance business, he was most anxious to make a good match so he hired a private detective to find out more about the girl's background and make sure that she didn't have a criminal record or any scandals in her past history.

At the end of a month, he received the agent's report as follows:

> Miss Simmons comes of a first-class family, resident in East Anglia. She has many friends and acquaintances in reputable social circles and has impeccable credentials. There is no evidence of any scandal in her past life. However, we have discovered that in recent weeks she has been seen in the company of a shady City businessman of very doubtful character.

A secretary had made a few alterations in a letter which her boss had dictated, and he was furious! 'You're not paid to correct my work,' he fumed. 'Just type out exactly what I said — exactly as I said it! Do you understand?' The secretary left without a word and the next letter she brought in for signature read as follows:

> Dear Mr Smythe — spell that with a y and an e on the end — the fool thinks it looks more impressive!
>
> In response to your letter of the . . . what is it . . . oh, look up the date yourself. We can offer you a price of . . . Jim, how much can we screw out of old Smythe on that machine tool order? £50,000? OK, we'll make it £75,000. Got that? That's a new dress isn't it? Very nice. A bit revealing but who's grumbling? Where was I? Oh, yes — if this price is acceptable,

please let us know within seven days. A deposit of £25,000 will be required to secure the contract − no, make it £30,000 − I don't trust him − he's the biggest crook in the business.

Yours sincerely, etc., etc., the usual guff. Now then, where's my coffee?

It was the annual general meeting and the managing director was in the middle of his opening address when the door opened and his secretary came in with a worried look on her face. 'Excuse me, sir,' she whispered, 'the treasurer wants to give his report. He's calling long distance.'

The manager of an engineering plant called a meeting of the works staff. 'We've got to improve efficiency,' he said. 'We've got to work harder. From now on, whenever I come down to the factory floor, I want to see every man hard at work. I am installing a Suggestions Box and if anyone has any ideas as to how this may be brought about more efficiently, will he please put them in the box.'

The next day there was just one suggestion in the box. It read: 'Take the rubber heels off your shoes.'

The boss was interviewing a new secretary. 'What sort of salary were you expecting?' he asked.

'About £200 a week,' replied the girl.

'£200?' said the boss with a smile. 'I'll give you that with pleasure.'

'With pleasure,' she said, 'it'll be £500 a week.'

The boss of a long-established City firm was very old-fashioned and set in his ways. When dictating machines were introduced for the first time, he refused to use them. Eventually he was persuaded to give them a try, but he was soon complaining that they were no good and that his secretary had not transcribed his dictation accurately. His secretary insisted that she had typed out exactly what he had said, and to prove it, she played his dictation back to him. When he had listened to the end of the tape, he shook his head disbelievingly and said, 'That's my voice all right – but it's definitely not what I said!'

The boss came storming out of his office in a rage. 'There are too many telephones on my desk!' he shouted. 'I've just been speaking to myself for the last five minutes!'

A party of business executives was travelling by train to London. They were joined by a stranger who claimed to be a mind-reader. 'I'll bet anybody here £100 that I can tell him what he is thinking about,' announced the stranger.

'I'll take that bet,' said one of the executives.

The mind-reader gazed at him intently for several minutes and then said, 'You are thinking of going to the City, buying £100,000 worth of industrial machinery, then going home, declaring yourself bankrupt and settling with your creditors at 10p on the pound.'

The businessman said nothing, but reached into his pocket, drew out his wallet, and handed over £100.

'Then I read your mind correctly?' said the mind-reader.

'No, you didn't,' said the businessman. 'But the idea is worth £100.'

The Lloyd's broker was somewhat surprised and annoyed when his application to join an exclusive business club was turned down. 'Never mind,' an acquaintance commiserated. 'They turned me down too. I got fifteen blackballs and there were only fourteen members on the selection committee. Apparently even the waiter didn't like me!'

The pit boss was interviewing a young lad for a job down the mine. 'Do you know anything about working down a pit?' he enquired.

'Oh, yes, sir,' said the lad.

'Do you know your gas regulations?' asked the boss.

'Well,' said the young man, 'I know it's Mark 7 for Yorkshire puddings.'

FIRST BOSS: 'How's your new secretary shaping up?'
SECOND BOSS: 'She's incredible! She's only been with us a week and already she's a month behind in her work!'

Personnel manager to job applicant: 'What we're looking for is a man with initiative, drive, enthusiasm and determination. A man with leadership qualities; a man who can inspire others. In short, a man who can pull the company's darts team up from the bottom of the league.'

The boss was saying goodbye to his secretary. 'I'll be sorry to lose you,' he said. 'You've been just like a daughter to me — rude, surly, bad-mannered and lazy.'

Just for a change, why don't you go in to work tomorrow, say, 'Good morning' to the time clock, and punch your boss?

A humble accountant came home from work one day in high spirits. 'Good news, dear,' he told his wife. 'The boss told me that he wants me to work in an advisory capacity, personally to him, at some time in the near future.'

'Did he really say that?' asked his wife disbelievingly.

'Well, not in so many words,' said her husband. 'He said, "When I want your advice, I'll ask for it." '

Two office girls were discussing their boss. 'Isn't he wonderful?' enthused the first. 'And doesn't he dress well?'

'Yes,' replied the second. 'And so quickly too!'

FIRST BUSINESSMAN: 'I really can't understand why your business failed.'
SECOND BUSINESSMAN: 'Too much advertising.'
FIRST BUSINESSMAN: 'Oh, come on — you never spent a penny on advertising.'
SECOND BUSINESSMAN: 'No — but my competitors did.'

After a prolonged strike in a Midlands car factory, the general manager was addressing a meeting of the work force. 'You will be pleased to know,' he announced, 'that the management have agreed to all your demands. Starting next week, all wages will be increased by 50 per cent, there will be twelve weeks' paid holiday per annum and we shall only work on Fridays.'

'What!' shouted a voice from the back. '*Every* bloody Friday?'

The sales manager of a large export firm received news one morning that one of his top salesmen had died in Milan. He immediately sent a fax to the Milan office: 'Return samples by airmail and search the body for orders.'

ASSISTANT MANAGER: 'But you can't fire me! Who are you going to get to fill my vacancy?'

MANAGER: 'Believe me, Sam, you're not leaving any vacancy!'

The managing director of a large import/export business was well known for his habit of always post-dating his cheques. In the course of time he passed away. His creditors got together and erected a fine tombstone over the grave. On it was inscribed:

HERE LIES ALFRED BOSTOCK. DIED 10TH OF JANUARY – AS OF 1ST OF FEBRUARY

A company director was being interviewed on TV. 'What procedure do you adopt when a really tough problem comes up on the production side?' asked the interviewer.

'We hand it over to the laziest man in the factory,' said the director. 'He'll find the easiest way of doing the job and then we simply adopt his method.'

The managing director of a large company called in a business psychiatrist to sit in with him while he interviewed three prospective secretaries. When the first girl came in, the psychiatrist asked her, 'How much is five and five?'

'Ten,' the girl replied promptly.

On being asked the same question, the second girl said, 'Well — I suppose the answer could be fifty-five.'

The third girl said, 'It could be ten — or it could be fifty-five.'

When the applicants had left the room, the psychiatrist said, 'The first girl gave the obvious answer — she's the straightforward type. The second girl said "fifty-five" and that shows that she uses her imagination. But the third girl gave both alternatives, which shows an ability for lateral thinking and the knack of considering all possibilities. Now which girl will you choose?'

'After due consideration,' said the boss, 'I'll take the big blonde with the tight sweater!'

| EFFICIENCY EXPERT: | 'I'm pleased to see that you've taken on quite a few new employees since I installed my system.' |
| MANAGER: | 'Yes, I had to hire them to take care of the system!' |

A chap was watching a gang of workmen digging a large hole in a busy street. The only man doing nothing was a weedy-looking individual who was looking on complacently. 'Street repairs?' asked the onlooker.

'That's right,' said the small man.

'Which one is the foreman?' asked the bystander.

'I am,' was the reply.

'*You're* the foreman?' said the first man incredulously.

'I am. And I'll prove it to you,' said the little man. Then turning to the nearest workman, he shouted, 'Flanagan — you're fired!'

A man called Dodgin was appointed foreman at a large Midlands factory. On his first day, hardly any of the work force knew his name. He was making his rounds of the factory when he came across four men in the corner of a deserted warehouse, busily playing cards. 'Who are you?' asked one of the men.

'I'm Dodgin, the new foreman,' he replied.

'So are we, mate,' said the workman. 'Sit down and we'll deal you in.'

The boss listened sympathetically as one of his young executives explained why he needed a raise. 'Yes, I quite understand,' said the boss. 'I realize you can't get married on the salary I'm paying you — and some day, believe me, you'll thank me for it.'

BOSS: 'No, I can't give you a job. There are so many people here after jobs that I can't even remember their names.'

APPLICANT: 'Couldn't you give me the job of keeping a record of them?'

'What are you doing on Sunday night?' the boss asked his attractive young secretary.

'Nothing, sir,' she said hopefully.

'Good,' said the boss. 'In that case, try to get in on time on Monday morning.'

The personnel manager of a large car works in the Midlands received a questionnaire from the Department of Industry. One of the questions was: 'How many employees do you have, broken down by sex?' He replied: 'With us, alcohol is more of a problem.'

A new secretary started work on Monday morning and the boss, who was a stickler for detail, said, 'Now, Miss Haines, I can't stress too highly the importance of punctuation.'

'I understand, sir,' said the secretary. 'Don't worry. I always get to work on time.'

Did you hear about the shortsighted employee who was working himself to death? He couldn't see when the boss was coming, so he had to keep working all the time.

The millionaire business magnate John D. Rockefeller once registered at the most expensive hotel in Washington and asked for the cheapest room available. The surprised receptionist said, 'But, sir, when your son stops here, he always asks for our penthouse suite.'

'My son has a rich father,' observed Rockefeller. 'I'm not so lucky.'

The boss was interviewing a young lady for the post of secretary. 'How many words a minute can you type?' he asked.

'Long ones or short ones?' she queried.

An ambitious young businessman asked a multimillionaire for the secret of his success. 'There's no secret,' said the magnate. 'You just have to jump at every opportunity that comes along.'

'But how can you recognize an opportunity when it comes along?' asked the young man.

'You can't,' said the millionaire. 'You just have to keep jumping.'

A fellow was struggling in a Birmingham canal. He called out to a passer-by for help and the chap on the bank shouted, 'What's your name?'

'Bill Hawkins!' spluttered the man in the canal.

'Where do you work?' asked the passer-by.

'At the engineering works up the road!' gasped the drowning man. 'Get me out of here!'

But the man on the bank walked off and made his way to the factory, where he demanded to see the boss. 'Do you have a Bill Hawkins working here?' he asked.

'Yes, we do,' said the boss.

'Well, I've called for his job — he's just drowned in the canal.'

'You're too late,' said the boss. 'The fellow that pushed him in has got it.'

The managing director of a large firm had a huge sign made up which said in bold letters: DO IT NOW! Within a week, three employees had asked for a raise, the assistant manager had run off with the boss's secretary, six typists had left to get married and the chief accountant had absconded with £50,000.

The millionaire managing director of a large multinational company approached the airline ticket desk and, laying a large roll of £50 notes on the counter, said, 'Give me a First Class ticket!'

'Where to, sir?' asked the clerk.

'Anywhere!' said the millionaire. 'I've got offices all over the world!'

A worker on a car assembly line was going round the plant with a collecting box. He approached a fellow in the paint shop and said, 'Give us 50p, Fred.'

'What's it for this time?' asked Fred.

'We're burying our foreman tomorrow,' was the reply.

'In that case,' said Fred, 'here's a tenner. Bury the whole ruddy lot of them!'

'Anything interesting happen at the office, dear?' asked the wife of a company manager as her husband returned home from the office one evening.

'Well,' he replied, 'I took one of those Aptitude Tests this afternoon and all I can say is – thank God I own the company!'

Many bosses believe in the theory of reincarnation. It's not surprising really because they see it demonstrated every day at five o'clock when their employees come alive to go home.

'My boy,' said the boss to his son, who was just starting out in the family firm, 'if you are to succeed in business, there are two things which are vitally important: honesty and foresight.'

'What exactly do you mean by honesty, Dad?' asked the lad.

'No matter what happens,' said his father, 'always keep your word once you have given it.'

'And foresight?' said the young man.

'Never give your word in the first place.'

Talk about eccentric bosses, there's a managing director of a North Country factory who has three personal secretaries — a tall one for longhand, a small one for shorthand and a midget for footnotes.

The chief accountant advised his assistant always to add up any column of figures at least three times before showing him the result. The following day, the assistant came into his office with a sheet of calculations and said, 'Here you are, sir — I've added these figures up ten times.'

'Excellent!' said the chief accountant.

'And here are the ten answers,' added his assistant.

The boss had a habit of taking any letters left over in his 'In' tray at the end of the day and putting them into his 'Out' tray. When a colleague asked him why he did this, he said, 'It saves time — and you'd be surprised how few of them ever come back!'

The chief accountant of a large City firm had a habit of coming in to work every morning, unlocking the lower left-hand drawer of his desk, taking out a small sheet of paper, studying it for a moment, and then carefully replacing it and locking the drawer. One day he passed away. The key to the mysterious drawer could not be found and the managing director ordered the lock to be forced. When the drawer was opened, it was found to contain a single sheet of paper bearing the words: THE SIDE TOWARDS THE WINDOW IS THE DEBIT SIDE.

The millionaire head of a large multinational was lunching with a friend. 'Why do you continue to work so hard?' asked his friend. 'Surely you've made enough money by now to be able to take things easy?'

'I'm just curious, that's all,' said the tycoon. 'I want to find out if there's any income my wife can't live beyond.'

The manager of a busy office was on his way to an important business luncheon and was in rather a rush. 'Quick!' he shouted to his secretary. 'Where's that list of people I call by their first names?'

A young bank clerk began to lead a conspicuously lavish life. He bought a Rolls-Royce, got all his clothes from Savile Row and started taking holidays in Monte Carlo, the Caribbean, the Far East and other exotic places. Finally, the bank manager decided to have a quiet word with him. 'Would you mind telling me,' he said, 'how you manage to lead the life you do, on £250 a week?'

'Well, sir,' said the clerk, 'there are 150 employees here and every payday, I just raffle off my salary at £10 a ticket.'

One of the most famous of Oxford Street's great department stores is Selfridges. When Gordon Selfridge was starting out in business, he opened a modest store and noticed that across the road was a large establishment with a sign boasting: ESTABLISHED ONE HUNDRED YEARS. Selfridge promptly had a sign of his own made up. It read: ESTABLISHED LAST WEEK. NO OLD STOCK.

'What I'm looking for,' said the boss to the job applicant, 'is somebody to do all my worrying for me. I'll pay you £40,000 a year. Think you can handle the job?'

'I think so, sir,' said the young man. 'But, if you don't mind my asking, in these times of recession, how can you afford to pay £40,000 for a job of this kind?'

'That,' said the boss, 'is your first worry!'

'Definitely not!' said the boss. 'I most certainly cannot let you have two hours off for lunch. If I did that, I'd have to do the same for every employee whose wife had just had triplets!'

FIRST SECRETARY: 'Does your boss pace round and round the office when he's giving you dictation?'

SECOND SECRETARY: 'Oh, no! If he did that, I'd fall off his lap!'

'Now, look here,' said the managing director to the assistant managing director, 'I don't mind you following in my footsteps, but I wish you'd wait until I get out of them!'

The boss was giving a pep talk to the latest recruit to the office staff. 'I run a tight ship here,' he said. 'I want men who are efficient, conscientious and hard-working.'

'Well, sir,' said the new recruit, 'I think you'll find I always give of my very best at all times.'

'That's what everyone says when they start,' said the boss. 'But how long will you continue to do your best?'

'I suppose,' said the new man, 'until I've got your job.'

'Off on your honeymoon, eh, Brown?' said the boss. 'Congratulations. How long do you want off?'

'Well, er, how long would you suggest, sir?'

'Don't ask me,' said the boss. 'I haven't seen the bride.'

The manager had been closeted with his new secretary for several hours. 'Oh, I almost forgot to tell you, my dear,' he said suddenly, pointing to her desk. 'If at any time my wife should come in unexpectedly, that machine on your desk is called a typewriter.'

The wife of a businessman who was frequently away from home was entertaining his best friend one evening. The lights were low, soft music was playing and everything was extremely cosy when suddenly the phone rang. The wife answered, turned pale and whispered, 'It's my husband! He's come back to town unexpectedly!' Her guest leaped to his feet in a panic but the wife told him to wait. After a few moments, she hung up and said with a smile, 'It's all right. My husband explained that he won't be home until late tonight. He's out playing poker with you!'

FIRST SECRETARY: 'Do you ever get nervous when you're alone with your boss in his office?'

SECOND SECRETARY: 'Yes, often! I'm always afraid he'll stop and ask me to take dictation!'

The seven-year-old son of the boss of a large advertising agency came home from Sunday School one day with a small printed religious tract. 'What have you got there?' asked his father.

'Nothing much,' said the boy. 'Just an ad about Heaven.'

BOSS: 'What do you mean, you want another day off? You've had days off for your honeymoon, your little girl's christening, your little boy's flu and your father-in-law's funeral . . . what is it this time?'

CLERK: 'I'm getting married, sir.'

A group of successful business executives were discussing their careers and the struggle they had had to make it to the top. 'It was particularly hard for me,' said one. 'I had to fight tooth and nail for everything. For the first few years, things were really desperate, but I never despaired. I just tightened my belt, rolled up my sleeves — and asked my father to lend me another £100,000.'

FIRST CLERK: 'I can't stand my boss. He's absolutely ruthless. I wish I knew what to do about it.'

SECOND CLERK: 'Why don't you tell him to listen to his conscience?'

FIRST CLERK: 'That wouldn't do any good. He never takes advice from strangers.'

The managers of two Blackpool rock factories met on the promenade one morning. 'You look worried,' said one. 'I am,' said the other. 'I had to sack my foreman last week. Instead of giving him a week's pay in lieu of notice, I made him work the week out. Do you know anyone who could use five thousand yards of rock with "Get Stuffed!" written through it?'

The managing director had just finished outlining his plans for 'rationalizing' the company and making half the staff redundant. He looked around at the assembled executives and said, 'We will now take a vote on my recommendations. Will all those opposed please signify in the usual way by saying "I resign".'

'About my request for a raise,' said the assistant to his boss. 'I think you ought to know that three other companies are after me.'

'Oh, yes?' said the boss sceptically. 'What companies?'

'Gas, Electricity and Water,' replied the assistant.

A very attractive young lady called at the reception desk of a large business organization and asked to see the managing director. 'Certainly,' said the receptionist, and then added with a knowing smile, 'The boss is never so busy that he can't find time to see a pretty girl!'

'Good,' said the caller. 'Tell him his wife is here.'

DOWN-AT-HEEL BOSS
TO BANK MANAGER: **'How do I stand for a loan?'**
BANK MANAGER: **'You don't — you grovel.'**

The managing director of an insurance firm was visiting one of his subordinates who was ill in hospital. 'Don't worry about the office, Jack,' he said consolingly. 'Everybody's going to pitch in and do your work — as soon as we can find out just what it is you've been doing.'

The boss was complaining to his wife one evening. 'That new assistant of mine,' he said, 'is really one of the most incompetent and inefficient people I've ever had working for me.'

'Don't knock him,' said his wife. 'It's people like him who make you look good!'

EMPLOYEE: 'Please, sir, could I have the next two weeks off?'
BOSS: 'What for?'
EMPLOYEE: 'My girl's going on her honeymoon and I'd like to go with her.'

The pushy salesman had managed to bluff his way into the boss's office. 'Do you need a good sales manager?' he asked cheerfully.

'No, I don't,' said the boss. 'Get out – I'm busy!'

'How about salesmen?' said the visitor.

'No!' said the boss.

'Well, how are you off for office managers, accountants, departmental heads, office boys . . ?'

'No, no!' screamed the boss. 'I've no openings at all for any staff at the moment!'

'Well, then, you'll certainly need some of these,' said the salesman, reaching into his briefcase and producing a large sign which read: NO HELP WANTED.

A boss has been described as a man who comes in to work late when you're early, and then comes in early when you're late.

WIFE: 'Did you ask your boss for a raise today like I told you?'

HUSBAND: 'No, dear. I forgot in all the excitement of getting the sack.'

The chairman of the board was reading the story of Cinderella to his small son. The boy was particularly interested in the part of the story which described how the pumpkin turned into a golden coach. 'Dad,' he asked, 'did Cinderella have to declare the coach as earned income or could she write it off as capital gain?'

'It's your wife calling, Mr Jones,' said the secretary. 'She wants to give you a kiss over the phone.'

'Just take the message,' said the boss. 'I'll get it from you later.'

BOSS: 'Now, Wilkinson, we are giving you a raise because we want your last week with us to be a happy one.'

A lot of people who think their boss is stupid would be out of a job if he were any smarter.

EMPLOYEE: 'Excuse me, sir, I've been working here for ten years and since I'm doing the work of three men, I feel I'm entitled to a raise.'

BOSS: 'Well, I can't give you a raise but if you tell me the names of the other two men, I'll fire them.'

As the office boy strolled in half an hour late, the boss said, 'You should have been here at nine o'clock!'

'Why?' said the office boy. 'What happened?'

'You look worried, boss. Is anything wrong?' asked the secretary.

'Wrong?' said the boss. 'I have so many worries that if something catastrophic happened today, I wouldn't have time to worry about it until next week!'

The owner of a large factory offered a reward of £100 for the best money-saving suggestion submitted by an employee. The first prize was won by one of the workers who suggested that the reward should be reduced to £50.

An insurance salesman was talking to the boss of an East End garment manufacturing firm. 'You should really have a Comprehensive Policy,' he said. 'It covers everything – fire, burglary, accident, explosions, floods . . .'

'Just a minute,' said the boss. 'How do you start a flood?'

Two bosses had just finalized a business deal. 'Now all we have to do is draw up a contract,' said one.

'We don't need a contract,' said the second. 'I've given my word, you've given your word – that's enough, isn't it?'

'It's good enough for us,' said the first, 'but we've got to have something to produce in court.'

JOB APPLICANT: 'I'd like to accept the post, sir, but the last place I worked for paid me a much higher salary.'

BOSS: 'But they didn't have a generous pension scheme like us, did they?'

JOB APPLICANT: 'Oh, yes – in fact it was much more generous.'

BOSS: 'And bonus payments and overtime?'

JOB APPLICANT: 'Certainly.'

BOSS:	'And six weeks' paid holiday a year?'
JOB APPLICANT:	'Yes.'
BOSS:	'Then why on earth did you leave?'
JOB APPLICANT:	'They went bankrupt.'

Receptionist, talking to customer on the phone: 'No, I'm sorry, the boss has just gone out to lunch. But I don't think he'll be long — nobody took him.'

It has been said that no man goes before his time — unless, of course, the boss leaves early.

| BOSS: | 'This letter is full of mistakes! Didn't you read it through before you brought it in for signature?' |
| SECRETARY: | 'No, sir. I thought it was confidential.' |

'I'm clearing out this filing cabinet, sir,' said the secretary. 'Do you want me to keep these old files?'

'No, you can throw them away,' said the boss. 'But make sure you keep copies.'

OFFICE RULES
RULE 1: The Boss is always right.
RULE 2: When the Boss is wrong, refer to Rule 1.

The manager's personal assistant was consistently late for work. The trouble was, he had the greatest difficulty in getting up in the morning. He took the problem to his doctor, who prescribed some sleeping pills for him. He went to bed early that night and had his first really good night's sleep in weeks. He felt so good that he actually got to work early. In high spirits, he said to his boss, 'I didn't have any trouble at all in getting up this morning.'

'Great!' said his boss. 'But where were you yesterday?'

BOSS: 'What's the idea of walking into the office at ten-thirty?'

CLERK: 'I'm sorry, chief. The cat got on the bedroom window-sill when I was dressing — I made a grab for it and fell out of the window. I was so dazed I wandered into the road and got hit by a bus, which dragged me three hundred yards down the road. I've just got back from the hospital.'

BOSS: 'I see. And this took an hour and a half?'

The managing director of a large advertising agency had occasion to visit his doctor. In the waiting-room he struck up a conversation with the man sitting next to him, in the course of which he asked him what line of business he was in. 'I'm in advertising,' said the man.

'What a coincidence!' said the director. 'So am I. How do you find things these days?'

'Not bad,' said the other man. 'But don't those straps cut into your shoulders!'

Smith, the director of a small clothing company, owed Robinson, one of his suppliers, £500. He borrowed the money from Brown, the director of another small company, and repaid Robinson. A couple of weeks later, Brown demanded his money back, so Smith borrowed £500 from Robinson and paid Brown.

A month later, Robinson again demanded repayment, so again Smith borrowed the money from Brown. This procedure was continued over several months. Then one day, Smith arranged a meeting with Brown and Robinson and said, 'Fellows, this is getting ridiculous. Why don't you two exchange the £500 every couple of weeks and leave me out of it?'

'What I need,' the boss declared one morning, 'is a chart that will show me exactly what charts we've got.'

The boss of a large clothing store was very pleased with his new sales assistant. One day he said, 'I'll be away on business tomorrow, Jackson, and I'm going to set you a real test of your selling abilities. I want you to get rid of that double-breasted check suit – the purple and yellow one with the wide lapels and the flared pants. We've had it on the rack for two years.'

When the boss returned from his business trip, he asked the salesman whether he had managed to sell the suit. 'Yes, sir, I did,' said Jackson. 'I sold it for £150.'

'Excellent!' said the boss. 'Did you have a hard time getting rid of it?'

'Not really,' said the salesman. 'I had no trouble with the customer — but I did have a hell of an argument with his guide dog!'

The boss was interviewing an applicant for a senior post in the accounts department. 'Have you any experience of double-entry book-keeping?' he asked.

'Oh yes, sir,' said the applicant. 'As a matter of fact, at my last place, I had to do triple-entry.'

'Triple-entry?' said the boss. 'What on earth is that?'

'Well, sir, we kept three sets of accounts — one for the active partner, showing actual profits, one for the sleeping partner, showing small profits, and one for the Inland Revenue, showing a loss!'

I want a word with you, Jones,' said the boss. 'Your salary is your own personal business and you shouldn't go around discussing it with any other member of the staff.'

'Oh, I wouldn't dream of it, sir,' said Jones. 'I'm just as ashamed of it as you are.'

FIRST SECRETARY: 'How is your boss to work for?'
SECOND SECRETARY: 'He's very bigoted.'
FIRST SECRETARY: 'In what way?'
SECOND SECRETARY: 'He thinks words can only be spelled one way.'

CLERK: 'Look here, sir, I've worked hard for the firm for ten years and I think I'm entitled to a raise.'

BOSS: 'But I gave you a raise only last week!'

CLERK: 'You did? I'm sorry, sir – my wife never told me!'

Proverb: Old bosses never die – they just sit around on their assets.

When the boss came into the office fifteen minutes early one morning, he surprised the office manager locked in a fond embrace with his personal secretary. 'Jones!' thundered the boss. 'You're not paid to do this, you know!'

'I know, sir,' said Jones. 'But I don't mind.'

Did you hear about the boss who was about to commit suicide when he discovered that the cleaning woman had hung the sales chart upside down?

'Collins,' said the boss, 'you've been doing such a great job here that I'm giving you a bonus. This is a cheque for £1,000. And if you keep up the good work, I may sign it.'

FIRST SECRETARY: 'My boss has a peculiar habit. When he's dictating a letter, he always kisses me to indicate a full stop.'

SECOND SECRETARY: 'My boss used to do that — but I had to put a stop to it. He kept putting in too many exclamation marks!'

'Get the telephone, Miss Summers,' said the boss irritably to his new secretary. 'I do wish you'd answer it when it rings.'

'There doesn't seem to be much point,' said his secretary. 'Nine times out of ten, it's for you!'

'I'm sorry we're having to let you go,' said the boss to his senior employee. 'But it may give you some satisfaction to know that the computer that's replacing you cost £100,000.'

Late one night, a policeman was checking a line of cars parked in a side street. He peered into the back of the first car where a couple were locked in a close embrace. 'What's going on here?' he asked suspiciously.

'Nothing, officer,' said the girl. 'I'm just teaching my boyfriend how to do the samba.'

The young lady in the second car had a similar excuse. 'I'm instructing my boyfriend how to do the rumba,' she explained.

The policeman shone his torch on the couple in the back of the third car, saying, 'And I suppose you're doing the bossa nova!'

'No,' replied the girl. 'I'm doing the boss a favour!'

'Miss O'Connor,' said the boss to his secretary, 'you have a very pleasant manner, you dress well, and you're very attractive.'

'Thank you, sir,' said his secretary, blushing modestly.

'That's all right,' said the boss. 'I just wanted to put you in a good mood before I take up the matter of your typing, your spelling and your punctuation.'

OFFICE BOY: 'I feel like telling the boss what I think of him again!'

SALES CLERK: 'What do you mean — again?'

OFFICE BOY: 'I felt like it yesterday too!'

The boss was looking over the books at the end of the month. 'You're supposed to show the profits in black ink,' he said to his head book-keeper.

'We haven't got any black ink,' said the accountant.

'Well, go out and buy some,' said the boss.

'If I do that,' said the book-keeper, 'we'll be in the red again!'

'Will you be back this afternoon, sir?' asked the secretary as her boss prepared to leave for an important conference.

'I may be back,' said the boss, 'and then again, I may not.'

'Right, sir,' said the secretary. 'Can I take that as definite?'

FIRST BOSS: 'Did you decide anything important at that conference in Bermuda last month?'

SECOND BOSS: 'Yes. We decided to have another conference there next month.'

'We've gone to a great deal of trouble to bring in this new efficiency system, Williams,' grumbled the boss, 'but you seem to be ignoring it completely.'

'I know, sir,' said Williams, 'but somebody has to get the work done!'

The boss's wife wanted to buy a very expensive hat from an exclusive shop in Bond Street. He managed to dissuade her by remarking, 'Certainly, my dear, you go ahead. It's a lovely hat. My secretary has one just like it.'

'Why do you always employ married men in your office, dear?' asked the boss's wife one evening. 'What's wrong with bachelors?'

'Well,' explained the boss, 'married men don't get upset if I shout at them.'

Two business partners were playing golf one afternoon when one of them suddenly said, 'My God! We forgot to lock the office safe!'

'So what?' said the other. 'We're both here, aren't we?'

The boss had told his wife never to ring him at the office unless it was urgent, so he was rather annoyed when she telephoned one day to say that there was something wrong with the car. 'What's the matter with it?' he said irritably.

'Well, dear,' she said, 'I think the engine's flooded.'

'All right, I'll take a look at it when I get home,' said the boss. 'Where is the car now?'

'In the canal,' said his wife.

'How's that new secretary of yours getting along?' one boss asked another as they were lunching at their club.

'She's either very stupid or very clever,' said his colleague. 'She's only been with me a week, but she's already got things in such a mess that I can't get along without her.'

'I hear you left your job because of illness.'

'Yes – the boss got sick of me.'

The boss was furious. 'Wilkinson!' he thundered. 'Come in here at once! What's this I hear about you praying in church last Sunday for a raise? You know I can't stand people going over my head!'

Every morning, when the boss of a large City firm went to work, he passed an old beggar selling boxes of matches from a tray slung round his neck. And every morning, the boss gave him 10p, though he never accepted a box of matches

in return. This went on for months until one day, on receiving his 10p, the beggar said, 'Excuse me mentioning it, sir, but matches are now 15p a box.'

Whenever they thought the manager was engaged, the four bank clerks started playing cards. One day he caught them at it. They didn't notice that he was watching and he decided to teach them a lesson. He rang the fire alarm four times, but the clerks ignored the bell and carried on playing. Two minutes later, the barman from the pub next door walked in with four pints of beer.

The boss had fought his way up from the gutter and despite being a very successful businessman he was no good at all at writing business letters. So, he hired an assistant to compose his business correspondence for him and then he just added his signature. This scheme worked well for a couple of years until the assistant left for a post with another firm.

The boss promptly hired another assistant to write his letters for him. On the first morning, when the new man brought in his letters for signature, the boss read through them with mounting frustration. 'This won't do at all!' he said. 'These letters are definitely not up to my usual standard!'

'Is it true that your boss is going to make you a partner?' 'Yes, I think so. He said yesterday, "Either you take an interest in the business, or you get out!" '

The boss of an engineering firm was looking to promote one of his juniors to senior executive level. He prepared a questionnaire which he distributed to all the likely candidates. One question asked: 'Have you any reasons for believing that you possess executive potential?'

One hopeful gave the following answer: 'I think I would make a successful executive because I never get lonely and I wouldn't mind working in a private office on my own.'

'Gentlemen,' said the office manager, 'I'd like to introduce the boss's son. He'll be starting at the bottom for a few days.'

My boss is such a high-powered executive, he has two desks – one for each foot.

The boss called the shop foreman into his office and showed him some elaborate specifications. 'We've got to produce a thousand of these by the end of next week. Think you can do it?' he said. The foreman studied the plans closely and then shook his head.

'Impossible!' he said. 'There isn't a firm in the country that can make a thing like that. We'll have to send out for them!'

'Boss,' said the foreman on a building site, 'the shovels haven't arrived. What shall we do?'
'Tell the men to lean on each other,' said the boss.

An East End tailor bought a small shop and opened up in business for himself. He was undaunted by the fact that there was a large and obviously successful tailoring establishment on either side of his premises. Over the left-hand shop was a large sign saying: E. GOLDSTEIN. FIRST-CLASS MEN'S OUTFITTERS. Over the right-hand shop was an equally large sign saying: J. J. MOSKOWITZ. TAILORS TO THE MILITARY AND THE CIVIL SERVICE. The boss of the little shop in the middle put up his own sign which said simply: ENTRANCE.

There is a very exclusive club in Mayfair which is popular among senior executives and top business bosses. For many years it was strictly men only – ladies were not allowed in under any circumstances. One evening, one of the top bosses walked in and was horrified to see that the dining room was full of chattering members of the fair sex. 'What's going on?' he demanded of the club secretary.

'We've decided in committee to allow the members to bring their wives in to dinner once a month,' said the secretary.

'Yes, but hang on a minute,' protested the boss. 'That's not fair! I'm not married. Supposing I wanted to bring my girlfriend in?'

The club secretary thought it over for a moment and then said, 'I suppose it would be all right – provided she's the wife of one of the members . . .'

Two partners in a small business fell into an argument. One of them had the bad habit of always using 'I' when speaking of business matters. 'Look here,' said the other partner, 'why do you always say "I'm going to do this" and "I'm going to do that"? We're partners, aren't we? Why can't you say "we" for a change?'

That evening he received a telephone call at home from his partner. 'I've got bad news, Morry,' said the partner. 'Our typist is suing us for child maintenance.'

FIRST SECRETARY: 'What's this collection for?'
SECOND SECRETARY: 'It's for Sally. She's not getting married or leaving or anything. She just feels she's stuck here for the rest of her life.'

'What I'm looking for,' said the boss, 'is men between the ages of twenty and thirty, with forty years' experience.'

A small-time businessman had been bankrupt on no fewer than four occasions. In the course of time, he passed away and when his will was read out, it was found to contain the following codicil: 'I would like all the bank managers with whom I have had dealings to act as my pall-bearers. They've carried me for so long that they might as well finish the job now.'

The ideal 'yes man' has been defined as a man who knows exactly how to tell his boss what he already thinks of himself.

In desperation, the boss of a large manufacturing company put up a big sign in the machine shop. It read: 'This is a non-profit organization. Please help us change!'

MANAGING DIRECTOR: 'Why on earth did you take on Wilkins as chief accountant? He's four foot eleven, he squints, he's bald as a bat and he's got a big black beard!'

PERSONNEL MANAGER: 'Exactly! He'll be easy to identify if he ever absconds!'

Have you ever wondered what a private secretary who marries her boss thinks when he rings up one afternoon and tells her he'll be working late at the office?

CLERK: 'I think I'm entitled to a raise, sir. I've been working here for twenty years — that's twenty years of valuable experience.'

BOSS: 'You haven't had twenty years' experience. You've had one year's experience twenty times.'

'Jones,' said the boss magnanimously, 'you have been working here now for exactly twenty-five years. As a mark of appreciation for your long and faithful service, from today you will be addressed as *Mister* Jones!'

The new secretary was obviously finding the work a little more difficult than she had expected. On her third morning, the boss asked her for some important documents relating to the current sales figures. An hour later, he stormed into her office and demanded, 'Miss Hughes, haven't you found those figures yet?'

'Hold your horses!' protested the secretary. 'I haven't even found the filing cabinet yet!'

CUSTOMER ON TELEPHONE:	'I'd like to speak to your boss, please.'
SECRETARY:	'I'm sorry, he's not in this afternoon.'
CUSTOMER:	'This is the third day I've tried to reach him! Doesn't he work in the afternoons?'
SECRETARY:	'Oh, no, it's the mornings he doesn't work. He doesn't come in in the afternoons.'

An employee who was leaving a large firm after many years' service asked his boss for a reference. When he got home that night, he thought he would just take a look at what his boss had said. The reference was short. It read: *'Mr Bingham has worked for me for fifteen years and when he left I was perfectly satisfied.'*

The boss was interviewing a young lady for the post of private secretary. In an effort to impress him with her intelligence and expertise, she said, 'Among other things, sir, I'm very good at doing difficult crossword puzzles – in fact, I've won many prizes.'

'That's very interesting,' said the boss, 'but I'm looking for someone who can be smart during office hours.'

'Oh,' said the young lady, 'this was during office hours!'

'Now then,' said the personnel manager, 'I think that just about covers everything. Do you have any questions you'd like to ask me, Miss Simmons, before I confirm your appointment?'

'Just one,' said the new secretary. 'You say there are 143 female office staff. Do they take up a collection every time one of them gets married?'

The manager of a large industrial company went down to the delivery warehouse and noticed a young lad lounging in the doorway reading a comic. He stormed up to him and barked, 'How much do you earn a week?'

'£120, sir,' said the young man.

The manager took out his wallet and said, 'Well, here's a week's pay. Now get out of here – I don't want to see your face again!'

The young man took the money and went off whistling cheerfully. The manager went over to the office and said to the warehouse foreman, 'How long has that lazy, good-for-nothing waster been working here?'

'Oh, he doesn't work for us,' said the foreman. 'He was just waiting for orders for take-away pizzas!'

FIRST BOSS: 'I'm really in trouble! In fact, I'm on the verge of bankruptcy. And the worst thing is, I haven't the faintest idea where I'm going to borrow the money from!'

SECOND BOSS: 'Thank God for that! For a moment I was afraid you were going to try to borrow it from me!'

BOSS: 'You're an hour late! Where have you been?'
CLERK: 'Having my hair cut.'
BOSS: 'What! On company time?'
CLERK: 'Well, it grew on company time.'
BOSS: 'It didn't all grow on company time!'
CLERK: 'Well, I didn't have it all cut off.'

'My boy,' said the boss to his ten-year-old son, 'one day you will enter the family business. You must be prepared for the cut-and-thrust of the world of commerce. Now I want you to climb up on top of the wardrobe.'

'Why, father?' asked the bewildered boy.

'Don't ask questions, just do as I say,' said his father. The lad clambered up on the wardrobe.

'Right,' said his father, holding out his arms. 'Now, jump – I'll catch you.'

'Dad, I'm scared!' protested the boy.

'Don't be scared – just jump! There's nothing to be afraid of.'

So the boy jumped – and at the last moment his father stepped aside and the lad crashed painfully to the floor.

'There!' said his father. 'That's the first rule of business — never trust anybody!'

The boss was interviewing three applicants for the post of personal secretary. His assistant manager sat in the corner in an advisory capacity. The first applicant was a stunning redhead who turned out to be an expert typist with many years' experience. The second girl was a lovely little blonde with a charming personality and she passed the shorthand and typing tests with flying colours. The third applicant was a middle-aged lady of ample proportions, with buck teeth, a squint and bad breath. Her shorthand and typing skills left a great deal to be desired.

When the ladies had left the room, the boss told his assistant that he was going to hire the third applicant. 'But why on earth would you want to do that?' asked the astonished assistant manager.

'In the first place,' said the boss, 'looks aren't everything. In the second place, I'm sure she'll improve as she gets into the swing of things. And in the third place, she's my wife's sister.'

A junior executive went to the office of the chairman of the board with some documents for signature. He found his boss standing at the window with his arms behind his back, gazing out in silence. Not wishing to disturb him, the junior left the office quietly.

A couple of hours later, he returned to his boss's office and was surprised to see him still at the window, staring out in exactly the same position. When his boss became aware of his presence, he turned slowly and said, 'You know, I can understand now why this country is in the mess it is. I've been watching those workmen down there in the yard and they haven't done a stroke of work for two hours!'

The Boss's Prayer: 'O, Lord, let me be Thy servant. Show me what to do. Guide me to my duty. Give me work to do – but, o Lord, let it be in an advisory capacity.'

At the funeral of the great automobile manufacturer, Henry Ford, his coffin was carried into the cemetery by eight pall-bearers. Suddenly Ford's voice was heard from inside the coffin. 'How many men have you got on this job?' he demanded.

'Eight, Mr Ford,' stammered the amazed pall-bearers.

'Fire six of them and put this damn thing on wheels!' said Ford.

'I understand you want to marry my daughter,' said the personnel manager to the junior clerk.

'Yes, sir,' said the young man nervously.

'Very well,' said the personnel manager. 'Let me have your application and include your name, address, experience and qualifications, and any other details you think would be appropriate. If there are no other suitable applicants, I'll ask you to come in for an in-depth interview.'

The boss of a large import/export firm had spent the whole morning dictating letters to addresses all over the world – Hong Kong, New York, Tokyo, Durban, Rio de Janeiro, Delhi, Melbourne and Toronto. Within half an hour, his secretary came in and said, 'I've finished, sir.'

'Good Lord,' said the boss. 'You must be a fast typist!'

'Oh, I didn't type the letters, sir,' said his secretary. 'That would have taken far too long. I just phoned them all up.'

A securities salesman telephoned the boss of a large company and gave him a very enthusiastic account of a new business equipment stock which he claimed was a sure thing and could be guaranteed to triple in less than twelve months. 'I happen to be the managing director of the company you're talking about,' said the boss. 'I'm glad you think so highly of us!'

'Well, what a coincidence!' exclaimed the salesman. 'Tell me frankly, sir – is the company any good?'

The boss had taken his secretary out to dine at one of the most expensive restaurants in town. 'What would you like, my dear?' he asked as they studied the menu.

'Well,' she said, 'I'll start with a champagne cocktail, some oysters and soup of the day. Then I'll have fillet of sole with French beans, followed by roast pheasant, baked potatoes, carrots, cauliflower and a side salad with garlic bread. French dressing, of course. Then I'll finish up with zabaglione, cheese and biscuits. To drink I'd like a Chablis with the fish and a claret with the main course, followed by brandy and liqueurs.'

'My goodness!' said the boss. 'You certainly have an appetite! Do you eat this well at home?'

'Oh, no,' said his secretary. 'But then again, nobody at home wants to sleep with me.'

EMPLOYEE: 'May I have tomorrow off, sir – to go Christmas shopping with my wife?'
BOSS: 'No, you may not!'
EMPLOYEE: 'Thank you, sir – you're very kind!'

'I hear you bought shares in your company,' said a colleague to a junior executive.

'Yes – and I wish I hadn't!' said the young manager. 'Now I lie awake at night worrying about the shoddy goods we're turning out!'

BOSS: 'Sanders, you've been drinking! I can smell it on your breath!'
SANDERS: 'Yes, sir! I've been celebrating the tenth anniversary of the last time you gave me a raise.'

'Mummy,' said eight-year-old Jimmy, 'can angels fly?'
'Of course, dear,' said his mother.

'Well,' said little Jimmy, 'when we went to see Daddy in the office yesterday and you went out to the toilet, I heard Daddy talking to that pretty lady who brought his letters in, and he said, "Thank you, darling — you're an angel!" When is the lady going to fly, Mummy?'

'First thing tomorrow morning,' said his mother grimly.

The chairman of the board had to make a speech at an important function. He was very nervous about this and as the moment drew near for him to speak, the toastmaster didn't help matters by whispering to him, 'Are you ready to speak now, sir — or shall we let them enjoy themselves for a little longer?'

The manager of a large City export house has a big sign behind his desk which reads: 'No — there's no damn reason for it — it's just company policy!'

SALESMAN: 'I've been trying for three days to see you, sir. Have you got a minute to spare?'
BUSY BOSS: 'Arrange a date with my secretary.'
SALESMAN: 'I did, sir, and we had a wonderful time — but I'd still like to see you.'

The Collector of Taxes recently received a letter from the boss of a car-hire firm which read: 'For the last three years, I have not declared all my profits and it's been preying on my conscience. I can't sleep nights. I enclose my cheque for £1,000. If I find I still can't sleep, I'll send you a cheque for the other £4,000.'

FIRST BOSS: 'How's business?'
SECOND BOSS: 'Terrible! Last week, I lost £2,000. The week before that, I lost £4,000. And the week before that, £3,500!'
FIRST BOSS: 'So why don't you give up the business?'
SECOND BOSS: 'You must be crazy! How would I make a living?'

A small boy asked his father, 'Daddy, what is a debtor?' His dad, boss of a big company, answered, 'A man who owes money, son.'

'And what is a creditor?'

'Ah,' said the boss, 'that's a man who thinks he's going to get it!'

BOSS: 'What's worrying you, Palmer?'
EMPLOYEE: 'Automation, sir. I'm afraid I'm going to be replaced by a machine.'
BOSS: 'Don't worry. They haven't invented a machine yet that does absolutely nothing!'

'I hear you have a special incentive plan here, sir,' said the new employee.

'That's right,' said the boss. 'We fire at the drop of a hat!'

A business executive was called upon to make a speech at a forthcoming dinner for top bosses. 'I don't know

what I'm going to do,' he confessed to a colleague. 'I haven't the faintest idea what to talk about.'

'Why don't you talk about sex?' suggested his friend. 'That always goes down well.'

So the executive gave a speech on the subject of sex and it went down very well indeed. When he got home that night, his wife asked him how his talk had gone. 'I think they liked it,' he said non-committally.

'And what did you talk about, dear?' asked his wife.

Not wishing to embarrass her, he said, 'Oh – er – I talked about yachting.'

The following week, the wife was approached by one of her husband's colleagues at a party. 'Smashing speech your husband made last week!' he enthused. 'I didn't know he was such an expert on the subject!'

'No, it's funny, that,' said the wife. 'He's only tried it twice – the first time he was sick and the second time his hat blew off!'

Did you hear about the secretary who was in charge of ordering the new furnishings for the boss's office? He had her on the carpet because she'd forgotten to order a new studio couch.

RECEPTIONIST (who has been told what to say):
'I'm very sorry, madam, but Mr Barker has gone to lunch with his wife.'

WIFE:
'Oh, I see! Well, when he returns to the office, tell him his secretary called in to see him!'

The boss of a small store in a country town hired a boy to sweep up and run errands. The lad was ambitious and thought that if he was to get on, he should be polite and friendly to his boss. On his second morning, he walked into the store and said cheerfully, 'Good morning, sir! Lovely weather we're having!'

'What's all this "we" business?' said the boss crossly. 'Since when is your name on the sign?'

'You're looking worried, dear,' said the wife of a top executive one night at dinner. 'Is anything wrong?'

'Nothing at all,' said the boss. 'I'm very optimistic about the future of the company.'

'Then why are you looking so anxious?' asked his wife.

'Because I'm not sure my optimism is justified!'

Two dress manufacturers met on the street. 'I see you're still selling your suits cheaper than I am,' said one. 'How do you do it? How can you possibly undercut me? Why, I steal the material I make my suits from!'

'There you are then!' said the second boss. 'You've got too many overheads! I steal the finished articles!'

MANAGER: 'Miss Young, I hear you've just become engaged to my son. Why didn't you come to me first?'

SECRETARY: 'I thought about it, sir, but I decided I liked him better.'

You just can't win, can you? Last week, I got into the office half an hour early every morning. Today the boss asked me if I was having trouble at home!

A new boss was appointed to a company that was losing money and going downhill fast. The board of directors instructed him to find out what was going wrong and put it right as quickly as possible. On his first morning, he made a tour of inspection of the plant. He asked the first man he came to, 'What do you do around here?'
'Nothing,' said the fellow.
The boss put the same question to the next worker he met and received the same reply: 'Nothing!'
'Just as I thought,' remarked the new boss. 'Too much duplication!'

Great Britain is still one of the only countries in the world where bosses can get together to talk about the recession over £75 lunches.

The managing director of a large organization called a junior executive into the office and said, 'I'm promoting you to chief executive, making you a partner and raising your salary to £100,000 per annum. What do you say to that?'
'Thanks, Dad,' said the junior.

'This recession doesn't worry me,' said the boss. 'I still owe £250,000 from the boom!'

'No, I'm not a religious man,' said the company manager. 'The Bible doesn't make sense. For instance, it says that the meek shall inherit the earth.'

'What's wrong with that?' asked his assistant.

'If that happens,' said the boss, 'who's going to collect the outstanding debts?'

'My boy,' said the boss to his son, 'if you ever have the misfortune to be declared bankrupt, always travel first class. That way you'll never bump into one of your creditors.'

It has been said that a business conference of top executives is like the mating of elephants. It takes place at a high level, it involves a lot of labour and it produces nothing for two years.

The boss of a large dress manufacturing firm was staying in a Midlands hotel and one morning he asked the receptionist if there were any fax messages for him. She told him that nothing had arrived. He asked the same question several times during the course of the day and each time he received the same answer. And then, late in the afternoon, the receptionist came up to him in the lobby and said, 'That fax you were expecting has arrived at last, Mr Goldberg.'

He read the message and then staggered back, exclaiming, 'My God! My factory has burned down!'

Did you hear about the assistant manager who went into the office of the managing director and said, 'Excuse me, sir, I've just received this memo marked "From the desk of the Managing Director", and I wonder if I could have a word with your desk about it?'

The boss had been away on business for several days. Shortly after he returned home, the telephone rang one evening. He answered it and then hung up. 'Who was that, dear?' asked his wife.

'It was a wrong number,' said the boss. 'Some fellow wanted to know if the coast was clear so I put him on to the Meteorological Office.'

The chairman of the board received a 'Second Notice' from the Inland Revenue warning him that his tax was overdue for payment and that immediate payment was required. He rang the Collector of Taxes and promised that he was putting a cheque in the post that day. 'I would have paid you sooner,' he explained, 'but I never received your First Notice.'

'Oh, we've run out of First Notices,' said the clerk. 'And besides, we find that Second Notices are a lot more effective.'

'I only have one rule in business,' said the boss. 'I never put off until tomorrow what I can do today. Tomorrow there may be a law against it.'

One company boss never has any trouble with unpaid bills. Whenever a bill remains unpaid for too long, he sends out the following letter: *'Your account is now overdue by three months. Unless we receive payment within the next 48 hours, we shall write to all your other creditors and tell them that you have paid us in full.'*

There was once a large firm of exporters called Smith, Smith, Smith and Smith. One day a customer rang up and said, 'Could I speak to Mr Smith, please?'
'I'm sorry,' said a voice, 'Mr Smith is in Brussels.'
'Then could I speak to Mr Smith, please?'
'Mr Smith is off sick today.'
'Well, how about Mr Smith?'
'He's in a meeting.'
'In that case,' said the caller, 'I'll speak to Mr Smith.'
'Speaking,' said the voice. 'How can I help you?'

The boss had installed a brand new photocopier in the typing pool and was becoming increasingly annoyed at its unauthorized and careless use by members of other departments. He issued a strongly worded memo on the subject: *'Staff are instructed NOT to interfere with the typists' reproduction equipment without my permission.'*

'Chief,' said the office manager to the boss one morning, 'I'm afraid we're going to have to get rid of that new office boy. Whenever I give him a job to do, he gets someone else to do it for him. He's lazy.'

'That's not laziness,' said the boss. 'That's executive ability!'

The boss's wife walked into his office unannounced one day and caught him in the act of eating his lunch with his pretty secretary sitting on his lap. 'What is that girl doing on your lap?' she screamed.

'There's a perfectly simple explanation, my dear,' said the boss. 'The pizza parlour next door forgot to send over a napkin!'

A cashier in a large bank called over the manager and said, 'Sorry to bother you, sir, but this customer wants to cash a cheque for £50 and insists on having it all in 1p pieces.'

The manager looked at the customer and smiled politely. 'Certainly, sir,' he said. 'Any particular dates?'

The proprietor of a rather dubious 'import/export' business was asked to come in for an interview with the Inspector of Taxes. 'What's this all about?' he demanded.

'You seem to be having some difficulty with your tax returns,' said the Inspector. 'It's really very simple. All you have to do is tell us how much your company has taken in, how much has been spent on expenses and what your total profits are for the year.'

'Blimey!' said the shady boss. 'I wouldn't even tell that to my partner!'

Sign seen in the office of a top business executive:

IF YOU CAN KEEP YOUR HEAD WHEN ALL ABOUT YOU
ARE LOSING THEIRS, YOU JUST DON'T UNDERSTAND THE
SITUATION!

Two top executives were lunching together. When the
waiter presented the bill at the end of the meal, one of
the bosses reached for his wallet and said, 'I'll get this.'

'No, no,' protested the other. 'We'll go Dutch — you use
your expense account and I'll use mine!'

My boss is a very generous man. Last week I asked him
for an advance on my salary and he said, 'Certainly.
How much would you like? Twenty? Fifty? Seventy-five? A
pound?'

The boss was welcoming his son into the business. 'I think
you'll make a success of it,' he said. 'But don't imagine
you're going to come in here and start at the top just because
I'm your father. You'll begin as a partner, just like the rest
of us did.'

Personnel manager to young lady applying for a private
secretary's post: 'We offer a salary in the upper bracket;
four weeks' paid holiday; insurance and pension plans; and
— as an added incentive — three unmarried directors.'

'As you enter the world of commerce,' said the millionaire business tycoon to his son, 'I want you to bear one thing in mind: money isn't everything. A man with one million pounds can be just as happy as a man with ten million.'

'This account is now nine months overdue!' said the boss of an industrial raw materials supply company on the phone to the managing director of a large engineering firm. 'I wrote to you personally over a month ago and you've never even answered my letter!'

'I never got your letter,' said the managing director. 'And, besides, I didn't like some of the things you said in it!'

There was once a very successful and enterprising clothing manufacturer who, despite his great success, had never learned to read or write. He couldn't even sign his name and his bank was quite accustomed to handling cheques signed with two Xs. One day, however, they received a cheque signed with three Xs. The bank manager rang to query the cheque and the boss explained, 'It's my wife. Now that I'm doing so well, she thought I ought to have a middle name.'

'Let me tell you something, young man,' said the boss to the insurance salesman. 'So far today I've had my secretary turn away seven fellows trying to sell me insurance.'

'I know,' said the salesman. 'I'm them!'

The boss invariably held his staff meetings at 4.30 on Friday afternoons. 'Isn't that rather an inconvenient time?' asked one of his colleagues one day at lunch.

'Not at all,' replied the boss. 'I find it most convenient. Nobody ever wants to get into a long argument with me.'

'Good news, dear,' said the boss when he arrived home from the office. 'I've at last managed to land that big government contract!'

'Honestly?' said his delighted wife.

'Let's not go into that now,' the boss frowned.

'What do you want a raise for?' asked the managing director.

'Well, sir,' said the junior, 'it's just that my kids have been pestering me ever since they found that their friends' families eat three meals a day.'

The boss's secretary was leaving to get married and the boss had taken up a collection amongst the staff and bought her a leaving present. 'Where can we hide it until the presentation?' asked the assistant manager.

'Put it in the filing cabinet,' said the boss. 'She never could find anything in there.'

BOSS: 'We can offer a private pension scheme, six weeks' paid holiday per annum, bonus payments every three months, a company

car, mortgage assistance and free health
insurance.'

APPLICANT: 'Sounds fine. What's the salary?'

BOSS: 'Good Lord, you don't expect a salary as well, do you?'

The manager of the local bank rang the proprietor of a small dress-manufacturing firm and said briskly, 'Mr Silverstein, your overdraft now stands at £950. You have made no arrangement for this facility and you've been overdrawn since last January.'

'What was the situation before January?' asked the boss.

'Well, you were actually £540 in credit,' said the bank manager.

'So,' said Silverstein. 'You say I owe you £950; before January, you owed me £540. Did I ring you up and complain?'

'Look here, Jenkins,' said the boss to his assistant, as they met at the coffee machine, 'you're drinking far too much coffee, you know. Caffeine is bad for you taken in excess — it can affect your work. Don't you know what the medical authorities say about coffee?'

'Yes, I do, sir,' said Jenkins. 'But I don't see what it's got to do with the stuff that comes out of this machine!'

At the annual shareholders' meeting, the chairman of the board was coming under attack from the dissatisfied stockholders who suspected him of engaging in fraudulent dealings with a government department. One shareholder stood up and shouted, 'I demand that you reveal the name of the sinister interest that controls you!'

'You leave my wife out of this!' the chairman shouted back.

A big business executive stepped out of his office and bumped into a group of colleagues. 'Coming to join us for lunch, Jack?' asked one.

'Sorry,' said the exec. 'I'm on the wagon!'

The company director was very keen on the subject of 'Delegation of Responsibility'. He called a meeting of all the departmental heads to address them on this topic. When they were assembled in the boardroom, he turned to his personal assistant and said, 'I don't think there's anything I need to say about delegation after all. You'll notice that all the departmental heads have sent their deputies!'

ASSISTANT MANAGER: 'Whose idea was it to put this ghastly vase of flowers on my desk?'
SECRETARY: 'It was the boss's idea, sir.'
ASSISTANT MANAGER: 'Don't they look nice!'

The office boy was called into the manager's office and charged with telling lies about the organization. 'Now

'look here, Jimmy,' said the boss sternly, 'do you know what happens to boys who trifle with the truth?'

'Yes, sir,' said Jimmy. 'When they get old enough, you send them out as sales representatives.'

Sadly, the personnel manager had died, and an ambitious junior clerk went into the manager's office and said, 'Excuse me, sir, I was very sorry to hear that Mr Jones has died — but I wonder if I could possibly take his place?'

'It's all right with me,' said the boss. 'If you can arrange it with the undertaker.'

ASSISTANT MANAGER:	'Sir, six months ago you promised to make me a departmental head.'
MANAGER:	'Well, I'm sorry, Morrison, there aren't any posts available. I'll tell you what I'll do. I'll set up a department to investigate whether we need any more departments, and you can be in charge of that!'

The boss was looking over his top salesman's expense accounts. 'What is this item here?' he asked. 'It seems a bit excessive.'

'Oh, that's my restaurant bill, sir,' said the salesman.

'Well, in future,' said the boss, 'don't buy any more restaurants!'

The managing director returned from a very long lunch hour and called his secretary in for dictation. After about half an hour, he said, 'Now lesh shee! How many lettersh have I dictated sho far, Mish Shmith?'

'Three, sir,' replied his secretary. 'All to the same person.'

FIRST BOSS: 'I hear you're looking for a new Head Cashier.'
SECOND BOSS: 'That's right.'
FIRST BOSS: 'But didn't you just hire a new cashier last month?'
SECOND BOSS: 'Yes – that's the one we're looking for!'

Just as the boss was about to leave for the office, his wife handed him a small parcel. 'What's this, dear?' he asked. 'It's hair restorer,' she replied.

'But I'm not going bald,' said the boss. 'What do I need this for?'

'It's not for you,' said his wife. 'It's for your secretary. Her hair keeps coming out on your jacket.'

The boss's wife answered the doorbell one afternoon to find her husband's secretary standing on the step. 'What is it?' asked the wife.

'I'm sorry to have to tell you that your husband is dead,' said the secretary. The wife gasped and then recovered herself with an effort.

'How did it happen?' she asked calmly.

'I'm glad you're taking it so well,' said the secretary with a smile. 'Actually, your husband is alive and well. It's just that he's lost all his money on the stock market and he wanted me to break the news to you gently.'

One of our top industrialists had a large number of signs made up which consisted of only one word in very large letters: THINK. He stuck these up all over his factories and offices. He was never able to discover the identity of the employee who added the words OR THWIM to every sign at head office.

'Shall I put this memo to all staff up on the notice board, sir?' asked the secretary.

'No, put it on the office clock,' said the boss. 'I want everybody to see it.'

FIRST WORKER: 'How did the boss take it when you told him you were leaving next week?'

SECOND WORKER: 'He was furious! He thought it was this week!'

The sales manager was interviewing a girl who had applied for a post in the department. 'You need to be good at figures for this job,' he said. 'How's your mental arithmetic?'

'Pardon?' said the girl. The sales manager sighed.

'I'll give you a simple test,' he said. 'If you buy something for £19.50 and sell it for £22.10, do you make a profit or a loss?'

The girl thought for a moment and then said, 'Well, I'd make a profit on the pounds but I'd lose on the pence.'

A young man barged into the manager's office and said breezily, 'Have you got an opening for a bright young man?'

'Yes, we have,' said the boss. 'Don't slam it on your way out.'

The boss was finally forced to admit to his wife that he had a girlfriend – one of the chorus girls at the local nightclub. His wife insisted on seeing the girl so the boss took her along one night to see the show. 'The one on the end is the sales manager's girlfriend,' whispered the boss when the show started. 'The blonde on the other end belongs to the personnel manager. The redhead in the middle is my girlfriend.'

The wife watched the dancers in silence for a few moments and then said, 'Do you know, I think I like ours best.'

Two office clerks were chatting over lunch. 'You know,' said one, 'the boss is really a very kind and thoughtful man. What can you say about a man who, seeing one of his office staff waiting for a bus in the rain, stops his Rolls and offers a lift; takes the clerk home for dinner; lets the employee stay the night; and offers the use of his car to get to work the next morning instead of waiting for the bus?'

'You mean to say that all this happened to you?' asked his friend in amazement.

'Not to me, no,' said the first clerk. 'But it did to my sister.'

The owner of a small firm of suppliers which was struggling to keep afloat had been trying for several months to obtain payment from another small firm without success. In the end he sent a final reminder and with it he enclosed a picture of his wife and four children with an accompanying note which read: *'This is why I need the money urgently!'*

A few days later he received a note from his opposite number enclosing a photograph of a sexy blonde in a bikini. The note read: *'This is why I can't pay you!'*

The chairman of the board had to make an important speech to the shareholders and, as usual, he delegated the job of writing the speech to his secretary. 'Miss Perkins, just put something together for me, will you. You know all the facts and figures. Write me something pithy and concise – about twenty minutes should do.'

When he returned to the office after the meeting, he was in a furious temper. 'What's the idea of writing me a one-hour speech?' he stormed. 'Half the audience walked out in disgust before I'd finished!'

'I wrote you a twenty-minute speech as you asked, sir,' said the secretary. 'But if you remember, you asked me to make two extra copies.'

The female boss summoned her male secretary into the office and said, 'I want to speak to you about your general appearance, Smith. How often would you say it's necessary to shave?'

'With a growth like yours, ma'am,' said Smith, 'I should say about twice a week would be enough.'

MANAGER: 'Can I count on your support in my application for the post of managing director?'

ASSISTANT: 'I'm sorry but I've already promised to support Blenkinson's application.'

MANAGER: 'Ah, but promising and doing are two different things!'

ASSISTANT: 'In that case, I'll be happy to give you my promise, sir.'

A clerk had worked for the same firm for ten years and decided it was time for a change. Accordingly he handed in his notice. A few days later, he met his old boss in the street. 'Have you got fixed up yet, Smithers?' asked the boss.

'Not yet, sir,' said the clerk. 'But I've applied for a post at Clarke and Dunham's and I think I'll get it.'

'Good,' said his ex-boss. 'I suppose they'll be writing to me for a reference?'

'I don't think so, sir,' said Smithers. 'They said that if I could stick working for you for ten years, that was good enough for them!'

Boss to employee about to leave for a fortnight's vacation: 'Have a good time on your holiday Briggs. Enjoy yourself, and when you come back, I've got something very serious to say to you.'

'Congratulations, sir,' said the young executive to the chairman of the board. 'Everyone at the stockholders' meeting was agreed that you gave a Rolls-Royce of a speech!'

'Why, thank you,' said the chairman, beaming.

'Yes, sir. They said you were well-oiled, almost inaudible and went on for a very long time.'

The manager of a large bank retired after thirty-five years' service and with his savings he bought a small garage in the West Country. On the first day after he had opened for business, a motorist drew up and said, 'Ten gallons, please – four star.'

Before he could stop himself, the ex-bank manager said, 'Are you sure you couldn't manage with five?'

A very powerful businessman had occasion to visit his doctor. After examining him, the doctor said, 'I'm sorry to tell you, you've got an ulcer.'

'Impossible!' roared the boss. 'I don't get ulcers! I give them!'

There were two candidates for the position of chairman of the board. One of them was pleading his case before

the selection committee and he said, 'I have served this company faithfully for over thirty years, at great personal sacrifice to my health, my other interests, my wife and family, my . . .'

'Stop!' said a voice from the end of the table. 'You've done enough for us! I'm voting for the other fellow!'

A shady entrepreneur had made a fortune by wheeling and dealing but had never had a formal education. Some of his envious colleagues asked him how he had managed it. 'I just follow a few simple rules,' he said. 'For instance, I buy goods at £500 and sell them for £2,000 – and I'm quite happy with 3 per cent profit.'

The new boss had only been in the factory for three months but he was beginning to get the distinct impression that all the work force hated him. He called in the shop-floor manager and said, 'Why don't the men like me? At my last place, they gave me a set of silver-plated cutlery when I left.'

'Is that all?' said the shop-floor manager. 'If you'd only leave here, we'd give you a solid gold dinner service!'

A company boss who had a well-deserved reputation for meanness and penny-pinching was accosted in Piccadilly by a beggar. 'Would you give me a fiver for a bed?' the old tramp said pathetically.

'Why not?' said the boss. 'Bring it round to my house and I'll have a look at it.'

'Did you post those two parcels?' the boss asked the office boy one afternoon.

'Yes, I did, sir, but you'd put the wrong stamps on them.'

'What do you mean?' said the boss.

'Well, sir, you put stamps worth £7.50 on the local parcel and a 50p stamp on the one for Hong Kong. But don't worry, I soon put it right. I changed the addresses over.'

The pretty young secretary had to accompany her middle-aged, balding boss to conferences and meetings all over the country and she was getting rather annoyed at the way he seemed to be treating her as his girlfriend rather than his secretary. They were dining in the restaurant of a hotel in the Midlands on one trip and as they studied the menu, the boss said, 'Now what would you like to eat, sweetheart?'

At this point, her patience snapped. She smiled sweetly and said, 'You choose, Daddy.'

BOSS:	'And how long did you work in your previous place of employment?'
JOB APPLICANT:	'Thirty years.'
BOSS:	'Hang on a minute! It says on your application form that you are thirty-two years old. How could you have worked there for thirty years?'
JOB APPLICANT:	'I did a lot of overtime.'

A management committee has been defined as a group of the unqualified, appointed by the unwilling, to do the unnecessary.

Two business partners were having a heated argument about the expense accounts. 'Are you calling me a cheat?' yelled one. 'Have you ever heard my honesty questioned?'

'Questioned?' said the other partner. 'I've never even heard it mentioned!'

Two bosses met in a bank one morning. They had just concluded their business when a gang of masked men burst in. Their leader shouted, 'This is a hold-up! We want all the money in the safe — and you people, empty your pockets and hand over your wallets!'

One of the bosses whispered furtively to the other, 'Joe — you know that £100 I owe you? Well, here it is!'

A man was lunching in a café one day and he made a call from the pay phone which was situated on the counter. 'Hello?' he said. 'Is that Mr Connell of Connell Enterprises? I wonder, sir — do you have an opening for a sales manager? You don't? You already have a first-class sales manager and you're very happy with him and he's excellent at his job? Well, thank you, sir. Goodbye.'

The owner of the café had overheard this conversation and said, 'Bad luck. I'm sorry you didn't get the job.'

'I already have it,' said the man. 'I am the sales manager at Connell Enterprises — I just wanted to find out what the boss thinks of me!'

The boss called his assistant in and told him that he was taking the afternoon off to play golf, leaving the assistant in charge of the office. When the boss had left, the assistant said to his secretary, 'As the boss won't be back today, I think I'll slip off early. I'll nip home and have a couple of hours in the garden with my wife.'

Arriving home a short time later, he was walking past the sitting-room window. He glanced in and saw his wife on the sofa locked in a close embrace with the boss. He ran quickly back to his car and drove back to the office. 'I'll never take a chance like that again!' he said breathlessly to his secretary. 'I was nearly caught!'

The boss was inspecting the site of his new factory where work was in progress. His Rolls had run out of petrol and the nearest garage was half a mile away at the top of a steep hill. He called to the nearest workman and said, 'Would you mind giving me a push to the top of the hill?'

'Right, boss,' said the worker.

By the time they arrived at the garage, the workman was, quite naturally, red in the face, covered in perspiration and panting heavily.

'Thanks,' said the boss, leaning out of the car window. 'Do you smoke?'

'I do, sir,' panted the workman, expecting at least a box of cigars as a reward for his efforts.

'I thought so,' said the boss. 'I should give it up if I were you — you're obviously badly out of condition.'

The managing director of a large engineering company which had a number of factories in the Midlands decided to pay a surprise visit to the Wolverhampton branch. The local staff were caught on the hop but managed to lay on a tour of inspection which seemed to pass off satisfactorily.

As the big boss was preparing to leave, news arrived from the factory floor that a lifting crane had collapsed and demolished several machines and a retaining wall, as well as injuring several workmen. Taking his leave of the chief, the factory manager said cheerfully, 'What a day, sir! Dreadful, dreadful! First you, and then the accident!'

A rough guide to those cryptic notes from your boss:

'*See me and give me the benefit of your thinking on this.*' ['I'm not taking the can for this one on my own.']

'*For your consideration.*' ['I can't make head or tail of it.']

'*Please note and initial.*' ['If anything goes wrong, we're all in this together.']

'*Let's take a survey among senior management.*' ['I haven't a clue what we should do — let someone else decide.']

'*Will you take a look at this and let me have an in-depth report in due course.*' ['If we can stall for long enough, perhaps everybody will forget all about it.']